THINK ABOUT
THESE THINGS

THINK ABOUT
THESE THINGS

Jane Merchant

ABINGDON PRESS

New York   *Nashville*

THINK ABOUT THESE THINGS

Copyright © MCMLVI by Pierce & Washabaugh

Library of Congress Catalog Card Number: 56-8742

Scripture quotations unless otherwise noted are from the Revised Standard Version of the Bible and are copyright 1946 and 1952 by the Divi-
sion of Christian Education of the National Council of the Churches of
Christ in the U.S.A.

Poems previously published are copyright 1950, 1953 by Abingdon
Press; 1952 by *The Christian Family*; 1950, 1954, 1955 by the Christian
Science Publishing Society; 1953, 1954, 1955 by the Curtis Publishing
Co.; 1949, 1951, 1953, 1954, 1955 by David C. Cook Publishing Co.;
1952, 1954, 1955 by Farm Journal, Inc.; 1952 by the Gospel Trumpet
Co.; 1955 by the Hearst Corp.; 1955 by Jane Merchant; 1955 by the
New York Herald Tribune, Inc.; 1953, 1954, 1955 by Pierce & Washa-
baugh; 1947, 1951 by the Progressive Farmer Co.; 1954, 1955 by the
Salvation Army, Inc.; 1949, 1952, 1954, 1955 by the Sunday School
Board of the Southern Baptist Convention; 1955 by *These Times*; 1953,
1954, 1955 by the *Washington Star*; 1953, 1954 by the Westminster
Press.

SET UP, PRINTED, AND BOUND BY THE
PARTHENON PRESS, AT NASHVILLE,
TENNESSEE, UNITED STATES OF AMERICA

PREFACE

Always, when I am reminded of Paul's message to the Philippians, "Whatever is true, whatever is honorable . . . think about these things," I have a sense of mental snarls being untangled, a homecoming recognition that that's what I should be doing, of course, instead of fuming about unlovely things.

I think Paul's singing text has this effect upon us all. We all have an instinctive awareness that "as he thinketh in his heart so is he," and that we cannot habitually entertain grudging, deprecatory thoughts and still live constructive, satisfying lives. We have all learned that thinking of the many excellent, pure, praiseworthy things in life makes the unjust, ungracious things seem less tremendous, and helps us deal with them in a better spirit, and more effectively.

The difficulty, for most of us, is in remembering what we know, and doing it. I hope very much that this small book, based on Paul's mighty text, may be of help to those who would remember, drawing them nearer to the One who gives us lovely things to think about.

JANE MERCHANT

Many of the poems in this book have appeared previously in periodicals. Acknowledgment is here expressed to the following publishers:

To *Adult Bible Class* for "Bounty," "Song," "The Source," and "Vulnerable."

To *Adult Teacher* for "First Snow."

To *Capper's Farmer Club Notes* for "Shepherd Remembering."

To *The Christian Family* (David C. Cook Publishing Company) for "Beneficence" and "Thanksgiving Prayer."

To *The Christian Family* for "Susanna's Apron."

To *The Christian Home* for "One Spacious Day," "Tenacious Is the Heart," and "Unequivocal."

To *The Christian Science Monitor* for "Gold Memory," "Industrious," "Maple Flame," "New Task Completed," and "Of Honest Laughter."

To *The Farm Journal* for "Curtain Calls" and "Delight in Duty."

To *Forward* for "In All Our Seeking."

To *Good Housekeeping* for "Meetings."

To *The Improvement Era* for "Lest Any Truth Be Lost."

To *The New York Herald-Tribune* for "Distant Star."

To *The Progressive Farmer* for "Birthday in Nazareth" and "Grandmother of the Hills."

To *Quiet Hour* for "God's Marvelous People," "Hitting Rock Bottom," "In Every Garden," and "Vacation Plans."

To *The Saturday Evening Post* for "Grape Leaves," "Values," and "Working Knowledge."

To *These Times* for "Prayer for a Son" and "The Little Prayers."

To *Think* for "Trust in Riches."

To *Town Journal* for "Because of Spring."

To *Upward* for "And God Said," "For Smiling Faces," "Glow in the Dark," "On a Hill," "Song While Working," "To Be at Home," and "Unless It Echoed Still."

To *Venture* for "For All White Flowerings."

To *The War Cry* for "A Prayer for Seeing Eyes," "Fulfillment," "Intercession," "I Will Be as the Dew," "I Wish You Christmas," and "Prayer for Our Laughter."

To *The Washington Star* for "A Song for Lonely People," "April Prayer," "Except One Child," "For a Good Year," "Hermann of Reichenau," "Not by Chance," "Of Courage," "Prayer for Mothers," "Remembering Ones," and "The Reason."

To *Youth* for "Camp Memory."

CONTENTS

I. Whatever Is True

1.	Think About These Things	11
2.	To Know Him Who Is True	12
3.	In the Treasury	13
4.	Hitting Rock Bottom	14
5.	Fulfillment	15
6.	"I Will Be as the Dew"	16
7.	For a Good Day	17
8.	For a Good Year	18
9.	Experience	19
10.	Lest Any Truth Be Lost	20

II. Whatever Is Honorable

11.	New Task Completed	21
12.	Working Knowledge	22
13.	Industrious	23
14.	Susanna's Apron	24
15.	Prayer for a Son	25
16.	The Little Prayers	26
17.	Song While Working	27
18.	One Spacious Day	28
19.	Vacation Plans	29
20.	Unequivocal	30
21.	Of Honest Laughter	31
22.	Prayer for Our Laughter	32

III. Whatever Is Just

23. On a Hill   33
24. For Smiling Faces   34
25. Delight in Duty   35
26. Heritage   36
27. My Mother's Sayings   37
28. Grandmother of the Hills   38
29. Curtain Calls   39
30. The Letter   40
31. The Crank   41
32. The Reason   42
33. To Be at Home   43
34. Because of Spring   44

IV. Whatever Is Pure

35. Except One Child   45
36. Birthday in Nazareth   46
37. Vulnerable   47
38. Prayer for Mothers   48
39. Shepherd Remembering   49
40. Glow in the Dark   50
41. For All White Flowerings   51
42. In Every Garden   52
43. First Snow   53
44. Values   54
45. We Won't Forget   55
46. In All Our Seeking   56

V. Whatever Is Lovely

47. Tenacious Is the Heart   57
48. Grape Leaves   58

CONTENTS

49. "And God Said"   59
50. Bounty   60
51. April Prayer   61
52. Intercession   62
53. Maple Flame   63
54. Muted Day   64
55. Trust in Riches   65
56. A Prayer for Seeing Eyes   66

VI. Whatever Is Gracious

57. Not by Chance   67
58. Meetings   68
59. Correspondent   69
60. Camp Memory   70
61. This Silent Hour   71
62. Gold Memory   72
63. In Sadness   73
64. Distant Star   74
65. I Wish You Christmas   75
66. Unless It Echoed Still   76

VII. If There Is Any Excellence

67. God's Marvelous People   77
68. Visitor to the Mountains   78
69. Funeral for a Son   79
70. Of Courage   80
71. The Source   81
72. Hermann of Reichenau   82
73. Remembering Ones   83
74. Afterthought   84
75. The Unnamed Four   85
76. A Song for Lonely People   86

THINK ABOUT THESE THINGS

VIII. If There Is Anything Worthy of Praise

77. Heritage of Gratitude   87
78. Song   88
79. The Sacrifice of Praise   89
80. The One Thing   90
81. Missed   91
82. In This Our Land   92
83. Thanksgiving Prayer   93
84. In Time of Harvest   94
85. Still Knowing   95
86. Beneficence   96

I. WHATEVER IS TRUE

Whatever is true, whatever is honorable, whatever is just, whatever is pure, whatever is lovely, whatever is gracious, if there is any excellence, if there is anything worthy of praise, think about these things.
—Phil. 4:8

THINK ABOUT THESE THINGS

There is no litany in the Book that sings
More tenderly than "Think about these things."
The mighty truths of God by which we grow
Are in it, all the verities we know
Of sun and seed, all certitudes of earth;
All honorable, honest work and mirth;
Soft whispers of the prayers of all the just,
True-hearted folk who make the Lord their trust;
The purity that blossoms in white flowers
And children's eyes, and falls in dazzling showers
Of snow; each lovely leaf and wing that lifts
Our hearts; each good report of gracious gifts
Of love and mercy; every smallest deed
Of excellent virtue answering daily need;
And all the constant blessings of our days
Forever worthy of our heart-felt praise.

All this the Lord our God has given us
To think and meditate upon, and thus
To grow profoundly, fervently aware
Of his unfailing providence and care.
This litany will equip our hearts with wings.
Leave doubt and worry. Think about these things.

God of all truth, help our thoughts to dwell on all things honest, just, and pure until our lives reflect their loveliness. In Christ's name. AMEN.

*And we know that the Son of God has come and has given us
understanding, to know him who is true; and we are in him who
is true, in his Son Jesus Christ. This is the true God and eternal
life.*   —I John 5:20

TO KNOW HIM WHO IS TRUE

If one of them remembered, Mary did.
If one of them said, on earth's longest day,
"Why are we desolate? We heard him bid
Us trust that he would rise, and show the way—"

It was his mother, surely. But they turned
Their pitying faces from her, and were still,
Remembering only the despair that burned
Into their hearts upon Golgotha's hill.

And so she pondered these things, through the night,
Within her heart, and through the night they shed
Their hopeless tears. And when, in dawning light,
They told her, "He is risen!" I think she said,

As mothers, since the world began, have done,
"I knew it would be so. I knew my Son."

Thou knowest, Lord, how frail our faith may be, and how we
doubt and fear when things go wrong for us and those we love.
Thou knowest how easily we are tempted to despair, forgetting all
past blessings and the truths that we have heard. Grant, our Father,
that we may so know him who is true that we may confidently
trust his words, holding them in our hearts till light returns. In
his name. AMEN.

Again Jesus spoke to them, saying, "I am the light of the world; he who follows me will not walk in darkness, but will have the light of life." . . . These words he spoke in the treasury.

—John 8:12, 20

IN THE TREASURY

These words he spoke
In the treasury:
"I am the light.
Who follows me

"Will not walk in dark
But will have the light—"
Oh, words new-minted
And shining bright,

Of greater value
Than all the gold
All the treasuries
Of the earth can hold.

All praise and thanks
To him be given
Who opens the treasuries
Of heaven,

And sheds upon
Our darkened way
The golden, pure
Life-giving ray.

Our Father, may we ever treasure the true riches, the words that bring us light and life and joy, which thou hast given us in full abundance. And may our hearts be ever generous to share, not hoard, treasures of truth and wisdom thou suppliest. In Christ's name. AMEN.

13

Every one who comes to me and hears my words and does them,
I will show you what he is like: he is like a man building a house,
who dug deep, and laid the foundation upon rock; and when a
flood arose, the stream broke against that house, and could not
shake it, because it had been well built.   —Luke 6:47

HITTING ROCK BOTTOM

"He's hit rock bottom," people say, of one
Who is beset by troubles, in despair.
Yet it could mean, as well, work well begun,
A digging deep with patient, earnest care
Until the firm and steadfast rock is found
On which a strong foundation can be laid
For a dwelling that can face the floods undrowned
And all the wildest tempests unafraid.

Those who come daily to the Christ, and hear
His words with all their being, all their will,
Not merely with the hearing of the ear,
And strive in all their living to fulfill
His words, dig their foundations deep and sure,
And in the stormy hours of loss and shock
That come to all, they suffer, but endure
Because their lives are founded on the rock.

God of eternal truth, grant that when we hit rock bottom it may
mean construction and not destruction. Give us wisdom to appreciate basic values in every area of experience. Let us never be de-
ceived by the allurements of the trivial, the shoddy, and the second-
rate; let us not build our houses on the sand. Help us, O God, to
dig our lives' foundations deep, and build on the eternal rock,
houses that will not fall in time of storm. In Christ's name. AMEN.

The mountains shall bring peace to the people.—Ps. 72:3, K.J.V.

FULFILLMENT

"The mountains shall bring peace." I had not found
Until today, the promise in the Book,
But these blue hills that graciously surround
My home, fulfill the promise, when I look

To them in any weather, any mood,
For they are always constant in providing
Peace for the cares that constantly intrude
Upon my heart, by their serene abiding

Through storm and tempest. Many times a day
When all seems transitory and unsure
I seek for that which will not pass away
To help me to be tranquil and endure;

And, like the One to whom I lift my prayer,
The mountains bring me peace, by being there.

We thank thee, Lord, that before we call upon thee thou dost answer, satisfying the needs of our hearts with the strength and the peace of thy hills, the breadth and the sweep of thy sky, and the profusion of beauty in thy earth. We thank thee for all thy fulfillings of our needs for worship and fellowship, for friendship and affection, for work and rest, for shelter and food. May we never forget that thou, and thou alone, art the unfailing source of all our good. In the name of Christ. AMEN.

I will heal their faithlessness;
I will love them freely,
for my anger has turned from them.
I will be as the dew to Israel;
he shall blossom as the lily,
he shall strike root as the poplar.
—Hos. 14:4-5

"I WILL BE AS THE DEW"

God is as dew upon the desert places
Where rain falls seldom, where the dew alone
Sustains and nourishes the tender graces
Of grass and herb; dew comes when light has flown

And all is darkness, as, in times of grief,
We feel God's cleansing presence close to us
And find, when light returns with sweet relief,
All things refreshed and gently luminous.

Dew comes when all the world is calm and still,
As God comes when our hearts are hushed and holy,
And richest on the valley, not the hill,
As God dwells with the humble and the lowly.

Oh, let us claim the promise, and renew
Our lives, for he will be to us as dew.

O thou who ever showest thyself faithful to the faithful, grant us
the faith to claim thy promises in our own lives. Forgive us, Lord,
our doubtings and distrustings that make thy word of no effect to
us. Remove from us our insincerities that keep us from complete
and sure belief. Cleanse us of all desires and deeds that make us
know ourselves unworthy of the least of all thy blessings, and
make our lives refreshed and beautiful. In Christ's name. AMEN.

The Lord is with you, while you are with him. If you seek him, he will be found by you.
                                                        —II Chr. 15:2

FOR A GOOD DAY

Waken softly,
Smile, and say,
"Lord of morning,
Lord of day,

"Thou hast kept us
Through the night,
Thou hast brought us
To the light.

"Thou wilt give us
Hour by hour
All we need
Of faith and power

"To serve thee well,
To do thy will,
In joy and sorrow,
Good and ill.

"Lord, we are grateful
And glad to be
Living another
Day with thee."

We thank thee, Lord, for rest and quiet waking. We thank thee that we may see thy glory in the morning as we lift our hearts to thee. May we begin each day with full assurance that thy resources of strength and wisdom will be available to us according to our need; may we not close our hearts to thy help by criticisms and complaints of what the day brings forth. In Christ's name. AMEN.

17

The land which you are going over to possess is a land of hills and valleys, which drinks water by the rain from heaven, a land which the Lord your God cares for; for the eyes of the Lord your God are always upon it, from the beginning of the year to the end of the year. —Deut. 11:11-12

FOR A GOOD YEAR

I am quite sure the coming year will bring
Perennial unexpectedness of snow
Dazzling my eyes with little stars that cling
A moment, to my lashes, when I go

On homely errands; and every year receives
For all the grievous things that come to pass
The myriad consolations of green leaves,
The myriad reassurances of grass.

There may be many burdens I must bear
And many challenges that I must meet,
But I am certain earth will still be fair
With sudden blossoms, brave and gay and sweet,

And all my past experience prophesies
Much gladness from familiar surprise.

We thank thee, Lord, for all the good experience of the past that brings us happy expectations of the present and the future. As in other days thou hast gladdened us with little blessings and encouraged us with diverse loveliness, and strengthened us to meet each challenge as it came, so thou wilt do in all the days to come. For the confident assurance of thy care we thank thee, Father. AMEN.

What I have seen I will declare.—Job 15:17

EXPERIENCE

What happened today?
The newsmen tell
The tidings so:
A government fell,

A statesman was killed,
An airplane crashed,
A city cowered,
Hurricane-lashed.

But here upon
This quiet street
An old, old lady,
Grave and sweet,

Handed a rose
To a crying child,
And sunlight sparkled
As they smiled.

I must believe
The clamorous, raw
News; but the smile
Is what I saw.

Lord, we would not close our eyes to wrong or be selfishly at peace while others are beset by disaster. Let not our hearts grow callous, we beseech thee, to news of suffering in any place. May we be ever responsive to need, seeking ways in which we can help. But, Lord, in a world where bad news travels faster than good, let us never forget that gentleness and kindness are also true. In Christ's name. AMEN.

19

Speaking the truth in love, we are to grow up in every way into him who is the head, into Christ, from whom the whole body joined and knit together by every joint with which it is supplied when each part is working properly, makes bodily growth and upbuilds itself in love. —Eph. 4:15-16

LEST ANY TRUTH BE LOST

If I should wound you, speaking what I hold
As truth in needlessly emphatic terms,
Expressing with a tongue too bluntly bold
For tact, conviction that my heart affirms,

Believe me, it is but my eagerness
To add to universal truth the grain
Of inward certitude which I possess
Through well-authenticated joy and pain.

For I am well aware no word of mine
Is all of truth, since truth is various
As individual hearts that must divine
Their own, and utter it with scrupulous

Swift zeal, aware of the exceeding cost
Should any particle of truth be lost.

O Father of universal truth, keep us from presuming that any finite minds can ever comprehend the whole of truth. Help each of us to bear faithful witness to the insights and convictions thou hast given us, and help us to respect the insights and convictions of others, knowing thou dost value the questing spirit and the sincere mind. Help us, O God, always to speak and act according to our understanding of the truth; keep us from great denials and from small evasions. In Christ's name. AMEN.

II. WHATEVER IS HONORABLE

Remind them . . . to be ready for any honest work, to speak evil of no one, to avoid quarreling, to be gentle, and to show perfect courtesy toward all men. —Tit. 3:1-2

NEW TASK COMPLETED

Now the new task is finished, and I plan
For other tasks more difficult to do,
This having given assurance that I can
Carry a more ambitious project through

To this glad feeling of accomplishment
In work done carefully, and not amiss,
That makes my heart creatively content—
Oh, I am always giving thanks for this!

And since the doing something new can bring
This happiness, and there will always be
New skills and knowledge for the mastering,
I marvel always at the folk I see

Who, listlessly unlearning, never know
The pure delight it is to learn and grow!

Our heavenly Father, we thank thee for the sense of harmony and completeness that is ours when we have done our work to the very best of our ability. We thank thee that the glow of satisfaction we feel when we have worked honestly and carefully makes it easier for us to be gentle, courteous, and at peace with others, because we are at peace with our own consciences. In Christ's name. AMEN.

Study to be quiet, and to do your own business, and to work with your own hands, as we commanded you; that ye may walk honestly toward them that are without, and that ye may have lack of nothing. —I Thess. 4:11-12, K.J.V.

WORKING KNOWLEDGE

A human being needs some pride in knowing
Some things that he himself can verify,
If it's no more than the proper time for hoeing
And planting beans, or how to still the cry

Of newborn things; he needs decisive acts
That keep his knowledge clear-cut and unblurred,
To hold him steady in the midst of facts
For which he has to take another's word.

Although it's fine to know the sun consists
Of hot atomic gases, anyone
Who crumbles sun-warm earth in his own fists
To make it right for seedlings, works with sun,

And, doing what he knows and understands,
Is proud of having knowledge in his hands.

We thank thee, gracious Father, for the quietness of mind and the clarity of vision which we find in doing with our hands the things that we can do especially well. When we are confused and troubled by the complexities of our times, grant us faith that every task done conscientiously is a contribution to the sanity and peace of the whole world. And may we verify this faith by our works. In Christ's name. AMEN.

This one thing I do.—Phil. 3:13, K.J.V.

INDUSTRIOUS

Sometimes when I am most preoccupied
With work, held altogether in its spell,
Forgetting myself and everything beside
In the endeavor to do one thing well,

The sudden lilting motion of a bird
Across the sky makes me aware once more
Of outward things, and I am oddly stirred
At seeing a world more vivid than before.

How good it is to pause a moment then
And savor to the full the zest of knowing
That I, as I return to work again,
And the sun shining, and the bright wind blowing,

And the bird writing music on the blue,
Are busy doing what we like to do.

Grant, Lord of grace, that every one of us may know the joy and fulfillment of doing the work we honestly like to do. Guide us, we pray, to the work that is meant for us, in which we can be happy, in order that we may be in harmony with thee and with all the works that thou hast made. If we dislike what we are doing, grant us to change either our work or our attitude toward it. In the name of Christ. AMEN.

He who is faithful in a very little is faithful also in much; and he who is dishonest in a very little is dishonest also in much.

—Luke 16:10

SUSANNA'S APRON

"I can plan better things," said Sue,
"Much better things than I can do."
And laughing, so as not to cry,
She ripped out seams that went awry
And sewed them neatly back again
As one can do when one is ten,
And wore the apron with a pride
Considerably dissatisfied,
Saying, "I did the best I could,
But it doesn't look the way it should."

I think that since Susanna's one
Who finishes what she's begun,
Who makes her fair and hopeful plan
And does the very best she can,
She'll surely some day find her seams
Entirely equal to her dreams.

Give us the grace of faithful perseverance, Lord, in all we do. Grant us to be on guard against the insidious effects upon our self-respect of leaving work half-finished or of doing it less well than we could do. Keep us aware, we pray, that every work, however small, to which we give our honest best increases our capacity for good and brings us nearer to the goals we seek. In Christ's name. AMEN.

Study to shew thyself approved unto God, a workman that needeth not to be ashamed. —II Tim. 2:15, K.J.V.

PRAYER FOR A SON

O Father, this I ask:
In every test
Help him to give each task
His very best.

I ask not that a host
Of gifts be his,
But that he make the most
Of all he is,

And that he never know
The sad futility
Of living far below
His own ability.

We thank thee, heavenly Father, that thou dost not require of us that our work be the best that can be done, but only that it be the best that we can do. As thou hast given varieties of gifts, grant each of us to value and use honestly the gifts that are our own, without envying or repining because others' gifts seem greater. In Christ's name. AMEN.

In everything by prayer and supplication with thanksgiving let your requests be made known to God. And the peace of God, which passes all understanding, will keep your hearts and your minds in Christ Jesus. —Phil. 4:6-7

THE LITTLE PRAYERS

The little prayers that people whisper low
And deep within their spirits, as they go
About their work, are seldom finely phrased—
"Lord, help poor Sarah, she's so sick and dazed
With grief—Lord, show her what is best to do."
"O Father, be with Tom and see him through."
"God, don't let children laugh at Jimmy's crutch."
"Give me the patience that I need so much."
"O God, I thank thee for the sunny scent
Of fresh-washed clothes that makes my heart content."
"Guide me, O Father, help me do thy will—"
Such short and simple prayers they are; but still,
Of all the little prayers that people pray
I doubt that any ever went astray.

Most gracious Lord, we thank thee that the little fervent prayers we whisper, hour by hour, bring thy sure help to us and those we love. We thank thee that though our prayer may find no words at all, the silent yearnings of our hearts and the faithful labor of our hands are prayers thou dost accept and generously fulfill. We thank thee in the name of him who taught us how to pray. AMEN.

You shall have a song.—Isa. 30:29

SONG WHILE WORKING

I'll sing a little song today
About a little road
That wanders where the willows sway
And little twinkling shadows play
And time is wonder-slowed.

I'll sing a lilting little song
About a road that lingers
Where weeping willow hours are long
And even those whose world seems wrong
Remember they are singers.

I wish that I were free to pause
From work and wander out it
Beneath green weeping willow gauze,
But oh, my work goes well because
I sing a song about it.

For all good memories of pleasant places, and for the songs that
make our work go well, we offer thanks, our Father, unto thee.
We thank thee that if we sometimes grow weary of the place
where we should be and of the work that we should do, our minds
can take small journeys to green pastures and still waters, and
return invigorated and refreshed. In Christ's name. AMEN.

27

Return, O my soul, to your rest;
  for the Lord has dealt bountifully with you.
  —Ps. 116:7

ONE SPACIOUS DAY

I am most grateful for a day with space
In it for noting, at respectful length,
The tenuous artistry of spider's lace
Spun on a bush beneath an oak's tough strength,

And for observing, with unhurried eye,
The slow unfolding of a passion flower,
And all the varied ways that cloudlets try
Of being beautiful, hour after hour.

The days when I have scarcely time to glance
About me, mid the things that must be done,
Are days I do not grudge, since they enhance
Appreciably, the joy of having one

Wide, spacious day with nothing much to do
But notice that my old delights are new.

Our heavenly Father, we thank thee for the good rhythms of work
and rest that bring harmony and order to our spirits. Grant us, in
our unhurried hours of quiet leisure, the ability to relax fully from
our responsibilities and cares, trusting the outcome of our work to
thee. And may we realize afresh thy bounties to us, and meditate
on them with grateful hearts. In Christ's name. AMEN.

VACATION PLANS

I cannot take long, leisurely vacations
In the green peace of some high mountain crest,
But I can give my often-voiced vexations
A long delayed and greatly needed rest.

I cannot take a trip to some far shore,
But I can give complaints a holiday,
And little irritations, by the score,
I'm packing up and sending far away.

The habits of being anxious, and of doubting,
And making tart remarks that need amends,
I'm going to give a calm and peaceful outing
All summer long; and when the summer ends

I shall be glad, indeed, if they should shirk
The woeful task of going back to work.

Dear Lord, help us to realize that when we are weary and irritable
it is usually less a change of scene than a change of self we need.
Help us to be eager to find loveliness in familiar surroundings, as
on vacations we are alert to see beauty in new places. Help us to
seek for and appreciate the fine qualities of those who are always
with us, as during vacations we are quick to find admirable traits
in the new people whom we meet. In Christ's name. AMEN.

UNEQUIVOCAL

I am not one of those who will not say,
"Winter is here." I will not say, instead,
"Summer is sleeping," when the trees are gray
And bare, and all the green of earth seems dead.

It is a time of resting, that is so,
And, being so, a needed time, and good,
A time of preparation, secret, slow,
For miracle in meadowland and wood.

But winter has a candid clarity
Of view, a richly formal, strict design
Of beauty all its own, in earth and tree,
And since I recognize as wholly mine

This chastened loveliness, not quite severe,
Why should I shrink from saying winter's here?

Give us, our Father, honesty and directness of mind, that does not
seek to evade reality by sentimental phrases, but finds the true
beauty and goodness that are in all the times and seasons thou hast
ordained. And if in our own lives, Lord, there are long stretches
of enforced rest that seem empty and unfruitful of any good, help
us to accept them patiently as seasons of preparation for greater
good, seeing in them thy design for us. In Christ's name. AMEN.

God hath made me to laugh, so that all that hear will laugh with me.
—Gen. 21:6, K.J.V.

OF HONEST LAUGHTER

The gravity of children, their intent
And firmly serious consideration
Of life, is the essential element
That makes their laughter reason for elation.

The laughter of the frivolous is shrill,
Ready at any cause, however slight,
And often seems a duty to fulfill,
A seasonless attempt to be polite.

How excellent it seemed today to hear
Not titters, giggles, or guffaws, but true
Exultant laughter, jubilantly clear,
From an earnest freckle-faced acquaintance who,

With unembarrassed dignity, refused
To laugh till she was honestly amused.

Father in heaven, may we ever strive for honesty and candor in all
our words and acts. Keep us from pretense, and from the little
insincerities that undermine our integrity and the genuineness of
our relationships. Give us, dear Lord, the humility and the courage
to be ourselves, and not to try to gain what is not ours by seeming
to be what we are not. May we respect others and ourselves enough
always to speak the truth in love. In Christ's name. AMEN.

Then our mouth was filled with laughter,
and our tongue with shouts of joy.
—Ps. 126:2

PRAYER FOR OUR LAUGHTER

Master of mercies, who hast given
The gift of laughter for our need,
Lest any heart be hurt, and driven
To loneliness, help us to heed

Most carefully, how we use thy gift.
O let our laughter, Lord, be kind
And gentle, having power to lift
The tired, discouraged heart and mind

Into the wider realms of being
As wings lift birds into the sky—
Let it not be stones flung, unseeing,
That stun a bird about to fly.

Lord, save us from regrets hereafter;
Keep us aware, through all our years,
That thou hast given the gift of laughter
For ending, not for causing, tears.

We thank thee, Lord of all good, that thou hast given us the release and the help of laughter. We thank thee for all who are of a merry heart and a cheerful disposition, who have the gift of bringing healing laughter to the careworn and the downcast. May we remember thee and honor thee, our Father, in hours of joyous merriment as well as in times of sorrow, and may we ever give thee thanks for all our joys. Through Christ our Lord. AMEN.

III. Whatever Is Just

He has showed you, O man, what is good;
and what does the Lord require of you
but to do justice, and to love kindness,
and to walk humbly with your God?

—Mic. 6:8

ON A HILL

"I need to be alone with God," I said,
And fled the nervous clash of will on will,
The tangled, taut emotions. But it seemed
A voice was speaking on the silent hill:

"Child, you can never be alone with God.
Those whom you hurt are with you even now,
The one your sharp impatience moved to tears,
The loving one whom you would not allow

"To help you with her wisdom, and the one
To whose necessity you gave no heed,
Being intent upon your own affairs.
They all are with you now, in all their need."

Deeply I prayed for them and for myself,
And rose with heart refreshed and love made new.
"Where have you been?" they asked me, and I said,
"I've been up on the hill with God, and you."

O God of righteousness, keep us from praying selfishly, and from seeking in prayer to justify ourselves to thee. Make us willing to hear thy voice, and to acknowledge the justice of thy judgments on our transgressions. We thank thee, Father, that as we confess our sins thou art faithful and just to forgive, and to create in us clean hearts, and renew right spirits within us. Through Christ our Lord. AMEN.

So if there is any encouragement in Christ, any incentive of love, any participation in the Spirit, any affection and sympathy, complete my joy by being of the same mind, having the same love, being in full accord and of one mind. —Phil. 2:1-2

FOR SMILING FACES

I love a smile on any face,
My mother's smile of tender grace,
My brother's smile of good accord;
Help me keep them smiling, Lord.

I love the happy smile upon
My sister's face, and any on
A friend's is like a sweet reward;
Help me keep them smiling, Lord.

I love each smile that I have won
From sad-eyed folk who offered none,
And smiles from one I had abhorred;
Help me keep them smiling, Lord.

Keep us, our Father, just and fair and kind in all of our relationships with others, that we may bring them gladness and not sorrow. Enlarge our sympathies and affections to include all lonely, troubled, and unhappy people, and all the unattractive, trying folk we know, and teach us to win from them, with gentleness and genuine concern, smiles of interest and pleasure. Through Christ our Lord. AMEN.

DELIGHT IN DUTY

It is, no doubt, the duty of a lark
To sing, the obligation of a thrush
In leafy sanctuary, to remark
With lyric syllables upon the hush

Of reverence that necessarily
Accompanies a sunset; and a wren,
In May, would surely be remiss if he
Should fail to utter rapture now and then.

It would be censurable indeed if one
With music in him should refuse to sing;
But oh, that men, like meadow lark in sun,
Could do their destined, their appointed thing

Without suspecting duty could be less
Than pure delight and perfect loveliness!

O Father, deliver us, we beseech thee, from coldness and lassitude
in the performance of our just duties. Transform and animate our
hearts, that we may do all the acts of service, praise, and love
which thou hast commanded us to do with zestful enthusiasm and
spontaneous gladness. Grant that we may wholeheartedly delight
to do thy will. In the name of Christ. AMEN.

The memory of the just is blessed.—Prov. 10:7, K.J.V.

HERITAGE

You ask about my dad.
You say you'd like to know
What qualities he had
That made folk love him so,
Why a workworn woman's eye
Grew bright, and a dark man's dim
When you spoke his name, and why
They liked to talk of him.
He was as deeply good
As trees and his own earth,
Helped everyone he could,
Not asking what their worth.
Always hard-worked, hard-pressed,
But always, always giving,
He never lost his zest
For laughter and for living.
His life was hardly such
A great success, some thought.
He didn't leave us much
Of anything that's bought,
But something more worth while;
After these lonely years,
A workworn woman's smile
And a weary dark man's tears.

Lord, we who have known the rich blessing of just parents thank thee for this priceless heritage, and we pray that thou wilt have compassion on all who have not known this privilege. In Christ's name. AMEN.

The tongue of the just is as choice silver. . . . The mouth of the just bringeth forth wisdom. —Prov. 10:20, 31, K.J.V.

MY MOTHER'S SAYINGS

"Can't never did do nothing," she would say,
Whenever I complained, "I can't do this."
And always I would find there was a way
To do it well, helped onward by her kiss.

"Cheer up, the worst is yet to come!" she'd laugh,
Whenever I bemoaned tomorrow's woes,
And ever since I've cut my grief in half,
Enjoying present good before it goes.

"Look at the little grass blooms," she would smile.
"Look at the baby sparrow, honey, look."
And so I learned to pause and gaze awhile
Observing things not found in any book.

And when my world collapsed about my head
She built it back. "We love you, dear," she said.

Our heavenly Father, thou knowest our hearts' deep gratitude for those who in loving wisdom have taught us good ways of living and of thinking. For all words that have cheered us when we have been discouraged, that have helped us to constructive attitudes, and given a sense of meaning to our lives in time of need, we praise thee fervently. In Christ's name. AMEN.

The path of the just is as the shining light, that shineth more and more unto the perfect day. —Prov. 4:18, K.J.V.

GRANDMOTHER OF THE HILLS

She always rose before the sun.
She watched the birth and death of light
For eighty years of mountain dawn
And eighty years of mountain night.

The mountain years are lean and hard,
But just and kind are all her ways.
It gentles one, she says, to watch
How God begins and ends the days.

What all the light revealed to her
I cannot say, but this I know:
Her face as latest evening falls
Is luminous with morning glow.

We thank thee, heavenly Father, for all people whose lives attest that at evening time there shall be light for those who have walked in the light of thy presence all their days. Help us to keep times of quiet communion with thee at the beginning and the ending of our days, so that our days and nights may be filled with radiance, and we may understand that each ending is a new beginning In Christ's name. AMEN.

CURTAIN CALLS

A little house I pass by on my way
Has curtains like a mist of April snow
That, airily, freshly dainty, seem to say,
"The sort of people you would like to know

"Are living here, the sort of people who
Love little homes, kept gaily spick-and-span,
And take delight in everything they do,
And give delight, as happy people can."

How glad I am for every house I pass
With curtains petal-bright or zephyr-thin
Drawn gracefully away from sparkling glass
That lets the sunlight out as well as in;

Each house whose curtains seem to call to me,
"Contented people live here; come and see."

Lord of all homes where families dwell in love and cheer, we thank thee for the blessing such homes are to all mankind. We thank thee for all homes where, in the security of their parents' faithful love, children are taught thy ways of justice, truth, and kindness; for all homes where aged people live in honored peace; for all homes where those who are weary with the labors of the day find rest and understanding. May all our homes deserve thy blessing, Lord, and may thy blessing rest on all who enter them. In Christ's name. AMEN.

Justice, and only justice, you shall follow.—Deut. 16:20

THE LETTER

I'd never seen Kay cry, not even the day
The doctors told her they could do no more;
But she was crying now. A letter lay
Crumpled upon her table near the door.
"Tell me," I begged. She tried to hide her tears,
Looking at me suspiciously, with dread.
But the hurt went too deep. "You know, for years
I've helped hand weavers out, by mail," she said.
I knew how eagerly she worked, indeed,
To gather patterns, news of special sales,
And good materials, for any in need
Of help, who could not pay for these details.
"It's something useful, though I'm crippled so,"
She said. "This lady wrote for my advice,
And soon was selling scarves, and all aglow—
She seemed extremely grateful, very nice.
Now she writes how a dealer tried to cheat—
She thinks; his payments were a little late.
She says, 'A Jew, of course—how he did bleat
And promise me the money if I'd wait
Awhile! Imagine thinking anyone
Would trust his kind as far as he could see!
There's not a decent Jew beneath the sun—' "
Kay dropped the letter and looked up at me.
"I don't believe she'd feel that way—do you?—
If I had ever mentioned I'm a Jew."

Lord, open the eyes of all who cherish prejudice and suspicion, that they may repent of the cruel evil of their unjust ways. Amen.

Then Isaiah said to Hezekiah, "Hear the word of the Lord:
Behold, the days are coming, when all that is in your house, and
that which your fathers have stored up till this day, shall be carried
[away]." . . . Then said Hezekiah to Isaiah, "The word of the
Lord which you have spoken is good." For he thought, "Why not,
if there will be peace and security in my days?"

—II Kings 20:16-17, 19

THE CRANK

"No doubt the townfolks told you I'm a crank,"
The lean man said. "Because I try to stir
Them up to act about the way our streams,
So clear and sparkling once, are being poisoned
With factory wastes; the way they're running mud
From hills with all the Lord's good trees cut out
And not replanted, left to wash away;
About the way farm folks who love the land
And try to use it as a trust from God
For future generations, get pushed off
By absent owners who make quick cash crops
And leave the worn-out soil to blow away—
What kind of heritage is that to leave
Our children's children, gullies, dust, and weeds?
Man, if you'd seen those people leave their homes—
It's not just soil, it's human souls we're wasting.
I try to stir folks up. They call me crank.
We are a nation full of Hezekiahs,
Good, decent folks who mind our own affairs.
'No matter what happens,' the feeling seems to be,
'Just so it isn't happening to me.' "

Forgive us, Lord, for causing desolation in the land thou madest
bountiful and lovely. Stir us from our selfish unconcern. AMEN.

When I look at thy heavens, the work of thy fingers,
   the moon and the stars which thou hast established;
what is man that thou art mindful of him,
   and the son of man that thou dost care for him?
Yet thou hast made him little less than God,
   and dost crown him with glory and honor.

                                        —Ps. 8:3-5

THE REASON

No one has ever taught me why
There should be quiet depths of sky
Unless for comfort of the eye.

And no one has explained to me
The reason for a reaching tree
Unless that strength of heart may be.

I know that sky and tree were here
Before man ever shed a tear,
Before man ever learned to fear.

But I cannot believe in chance
While in my darkest circumstance
The sky and tree reward my glance.

O thou whose universe is vast beyond the power of human minds to comprehend, whose creation seems ever more complex and marvelous the more we learn of it, we thank thee that the simplest of us may gain rest and comfort from the far depths of the sky, and strength from the upward reaching of the trees. We thank thee for all the things that minister to our needs, increasing our faith that thou dost care for us. In Christ's name. AMEN.

I have learned, in whatever state I am, to be content. I know how to be abased, and I know how to abound; in any and all circumstances I have learned the secret of facing plenty and hunger, abundance and want. I can do all things in him who strengthens me.
—Phil. 4:11-13

TO BE AT HOME

I am at home with winter.
I understand the thin
Determined trees, and all the calm,
Bare fields and I are kin.

I am at home with winter,
And I am glad to share
The dull gray days of waiting,
The cold, unfruitful air.

All hearts must master silence
Before they learn to sing,
Must be at home with winter
To be at home with spring.

Our heavenly Father, we thank thee for the justice and the equity of thy appointed seasons. We thank thee that every season, in its order, brings its own particular good. Grant that we may not miss the good our winter seasons hold for us; teach us that if we cannot be content with little, we can never be content with much. In the name of Christ. AMEN.

Thou openest thy hand,
  thou satisfiest the desire of every living thing.
The Lord is just in all his ways,
  and kind in all his doings.

—Ps. 145:16-17

BECAUSE OF SPRING

Because of dogwood's blessing on the hill,
Because of lilac odor drifting through
These lonely rooms, because of wings that fill
The vast sky's infinite extent of blue

With eager, onward joy—because once more
Earth grows more beautiful than I had dreamed
It could become again, my praises soar
To God, and I am stronger than I seemed.

I know I could not find a lovelier way
Through life's bewildering sorrows, than with the sight
Of dogwood blossoms, lilac's scented spray,
And April birds' exhilarating flight.

I find fresh courage for my journeying
Through every troubled year, because of spring.

We thank thee, Lord of justice and of kindness, that after winter, always, springtime comes, satisfying the desires of living things for color, light, and warmth. For all fulfillments of our faith in lawns and gardens, and for the quickened hope and freshened courage that they bring, we praise thee, Father, with rejoicing hearts. In Christ's name. AMEN.

IV. WHATEVER IS PURE

Even a child makes himself known by his acts,
whether what he does is pure and right.
　　　　　　　　　　　　—Prov. 20:11

EXCEPT ONE CHILD

It was the day of rest. No one came near
The sealed tomb where the guards paced up and down,
Except one child. "What are you doing here?"
A watchman questioned sharply, with a frown.

"I'm bringing flowers here," the child replied.
"My father and my mother are afraid.
They say all hope is gone, since Jesus died,
But I am bringing flowers, because he made

Me well, and he was fond of flowers and birds.
He taught me things. I'm not afraid of you."
The watchman stared, bewildered by the words.
"Well, run along—oh, all right, leave a few."

At last the long, strange night came to a close,
And Christ found blossoms waiting, when he rose.

Our heavenly Father, give us purity of heart and singleness of purpose in doing whatever we can do for Christ. Help us to remember all that he has done for us and all that we have learned from him, that we may serve him with selfless devotion, each in our appointed way. May we be wholly undeterred by others' doubts, and by fear of consequences to ourselves, from doing the things we know are pure and right. In his name we pray. AMEN.

Blessed are the pure in heart, for they shall see God.—Matt. 5:8

BIRTHDAY IN NAZARETH

Mary wove a seamless robe
Of her worship and her love,
All the softness of the lamb,
Whiteness of the dove.

Joseph made a shepherd's crook,
Rod of comfort, staff of care,
Meet to walk beside still waters,
Carved with rich designs and fair.

His brothers and His sisters brought Him
Tiny treasures of the field,
Curious pebbles, fragrant grasses,
Birds whose broken wings He healed.

Not all the gifts the world has given
Were touched with stars and angel's breath
Like those they offered, humble, eager,
At home in Nazareth.

Dear heavenly Father, we thank thee always for the child of Nazareth, and for the holiness and purity and love of the home where he grew strong in spirit, filled with wisdom and with grace. Help us, O God, to do all that we can do to insure that children everywhere may grow in purity and goodness. May we work tirelessly to save them from forces of greed and evil that would corrupt their minds and lead them into dark unhallowed ways. For his sake. AMEN.

For freedom Christ has set us free.—Gal. 5:1

VULNERABLE

I said to a child who had stubbed his toe
On a rock, "It wouldn't have happened, you know,
If you'd only consent to wear your shoes!"
And I thought, *I wouldn't have stubbed my heart
On a prejudice, if I'd worn a smart
Conformity to others' views.*

"But shoes are stiff, and they're hard, and hot!"
He said, and I couldn't well say they're not.
So I gave him a cookie to ease the pain,
And off he went with his brown feet bare
To rocks and grass and the summer air,
And the sudden delight of the summer rain.

And I wasn't really sorry to see
That he understood that it's best to be
Vulnerable, if we must, and free.

Lord, keep our minds from growing set in narrow, rigid ways. Save us from valuing conformity more than conscience, and the approval of our companions more than thine. Keep us from being silent when we ought to speak against prejudice, injustice, and unkindness, and from doing nothing when we ought to act. In Christ's name. AMEN.

You who seek God, let your hearts revive.
For the Lord hears the needy,
  and does not despise his own that are in bonds.
                                                —Ps. 69:32-33

PRAYER FOR MOTHERS

Thy grace to every mother;
And oh, thy special grace
To mothers of the children
Whose feet do not keep pace

With the running of their playmates,
Who do not hear, or see;
Thy grace to all the mothers
Whose wounded hearts must be

The source of reassurance,
Encouragement, and power
To children who are different.
Lord, give them, hour by hour,

Good cheer and faith and courage
And steadfast self-control
To help their helpless children
Grow strong in heart and soul.

God of compassionate love, we thank thee for the wealth of pure love and selfless devotion in the hearts of mothers. We thank thee for the faith which refuses to accept limitation and defeat, and the patient hope that persists when all others despair. We thank thee for all mothers who believe in the power of the spirit, and who help their children build good lives in spite of circumstances. In Christ's name. AMEN.

And the shepherds returned, glorifying and praising God for all they had heard and seen. —Luke 2:20

SHEPHERD REMEMBERING

Nothing has ever sounded quite the same
Since that strange night
Rang with a sound of stars, a song of flame,
A psalm of light.

Bird-music now is sweet beyond all knowing,
And any lullaby . . .
And I have heard the star-song re-echoing
In a child's cry.

But angry voices harsh with hate are stranger
And harsher still,
Remembering words that led us to the manger;
"Peace, and good will."

O God, who hast given us the pure, clear music of thy songs of peace, forgive us for the discords and the inharmonies among us. Forgive us for the hatred and suspicion that we as individuals, and groups, and races, and nations feel for one another, and grant that understanding, respect, and friendship may replace contempt and fear in all the relationships of persons and of nations. In the name of Christ. AMEN.

Look to him, and be radiant;
so your faces shall never be ashamed.
—Ps. 34:5

GLOW IN THE DARK

The little picture on my wall
Absorbs by day the tinest spark
Of light that touches it, and gives
A gentle glowing in the dark.

And when I waken in the night
And see its reassuring ray
Shine through the gloom, it always seems
More lovely even than by day.

Oh, may our spirits so respond
To radiance of the Father's power
In sunny days, that they may glow
Steadfastly in the darkest hour.

Lord of radiance, grant that there may be in us no darkness of self-will, no clouds of complaint and repining, to keep thy radiance from reaching us, and from reaching others through us. May we ever look steadfastly unto thee; let thy pure light illuminate our minds with thoughts of truth and wisdom, and inspire our hearts to acts of helpful love. In Christ's name. AMEN.

Blessed by the Lord be his land,
  with the choicest gifts of heaven above,

. . . .

with the best gifts of the earth and its fulness,
  and the favor of him that dwelt in the bush.
                    —Deut. 33:13-16

FOR ALL WHITE FLOWERINGS

For all the fair white flowerings
Of petaled innocence there are
I thank thee with the joy that sings
Within my heart; for every Star

Of Bethlehem, for every pure
White loveliness of lily grace,
And every pear tree's white allure
That makes a hill a hallowed place.

I have been glad for every hue
Of color any petals show,
For purple, yellow, crimson, blue;
And yet I shall forever owe

My heart's most reverent delight
To all earth's flowerings of white.

Lord of our lives, we thank thee for the flowers whose stainless purity speaks to our hearts of thee, and of thy demand on us for perfect purity in all our thoughts and words and deeds. May our minds be so filled with reverent love and thankfulness for all that is holy, pure, and lovely that there can be no place in them for evil imaginations and desires. In Christ's name. AMEN.

He went forth with his disciples across the Kidron valley, where there was a garden. —John 18:1

IN EVERY GARDEN

In every garden, plant a passion flower,
The flower of sorrowful, strange loveliness
That blossoms for a brief and wistful hour
Bearing the implements of all distress,

The nails, the hammer, and the crown of thorn,
Above a wound-red center, and above
Frail petals colored like the robe of scorn
With which men mocked the suffering King of love.

In every garden there should be a place
For beauty symbolizing pain and pardon,
The grave and gentle signature of grace.
Oh, plant a passion flower in every garden,

That men may hold in reverent memory,
Always, the Garden of Gethsemane.

Dear Lord, we thank thee for all the gentle legends of the flowers of the passion flower that symbolizes the passion of the Savior of the dogwood whose blossoms bear the crown of thorn and the print of nails, and the cereus that shows the manger and the star. We thank thee for the legends that express the closeness men have ever felt, among the growing things that thou hast made, to thee and to thy love. We thank thee in Christ's name. AMEN.

Have you entered the storehouses of the snow?—Job 38:22

FIRST SNOW

No one is old
Who lifts his eyes
And sees descend
From busy skies

The season's first
White flakes of cold.
Whatever his age,
He is not old,

Because he knows
One heaven-sent
Moment of pure
Astonishment.

We thank thee, heavenly Father, for the swift, pure loveliness of falling snow that makes us young again with wonder and delight. We thank thee for all the myriad unexpected ways in which thou dost surprise our eyes with beauty, so that we forget for a moment our small preoccupations, exulting in the works that thou hast wrought. In Christ's name. AMEN.

Look not every man on his own things, but every man also on the things of others. —Phil. 2:4, K.J.V.

VALUES

The most uncluttered spirit clings
Tenaciously to certain things;

A row of books upon a shelf
May seem the essence of oneself,

Or box of faded papers be
Assurance of identity—

For each, some things are set apart
Whose loss would mutilate the heart.

Yet some, who would not aim a blow
To injure anyone they know,

May often be so blindly rash
They call another's treasures trash.

Father in heaven, forgive us for our double-mindedness. Forgive us for judging ourselves by one standard and other people by another. Help us to remember that others' feelings and possessions are as important to them as ours are to us, and as deserving of respect. Give us, dear Lord, the ability to see other people's point of view, and to do to others, in all things, as we would have them do to us. In Christ's name. AMEN.

Religion that is pure and undefiled before God and the Father is this: to visit orphans and widows in their affliction, and to keep oneself unstained from the world. —Jas. 1:27

WE WON'T FORGET

Three neighbors sat at evening in our yard.
Soon Angie came. "I've called on newer neighbors."
"Oh—we should go," we said. "I'll say you should!
It nearly made me cry they were so glad
To see me—to see anyone come in.
The lady whose husband died four months ago—
She's had no visitors for three months past."
"Oh, no!" "I've thought each day for weeks I'd go,
But I thought surely other folks had gone."
"Don't count on other folks. They count on you."
"It's hard to visit strangers; they might snub you."
"Well, if they do, it's just your pride that's hurt.
That woman's very soul was nearly dead."
"Maybe we need a church committee—" "No.
We need the kind of individual caring
That makes a person do the things he should
Without being prodded to it by committees!"
Then Angie smiled. "I'm talking at myself.
Just say those words back to me every week."
"We will," we said. "If you'll say them to us."
"The little widow's coming over tomorrow,
She, and the Japanese girl Jim Brown married—
She's sweet, and horribly lonely. You all come."
"We will," we said. "Now don't forget." "We won't "

Lord, let us not forget or neglect to offer friendship to the lonely people in our midst. In Christ's name. AMEN.

Aim at righteousness, faith, love, and peace, along with those who call upon the Lord from a pure heart. —II Tim. 2:22

IN ALL OUR SEEKING

Lord God of all our seeking
For peace and brotherhood,
For love and grace and gladness
And all things good,

Preserve us, Lord, from seeking
Good for ourselves alone,
And those whom we have always loved,
Have always known.

O teach us that no blessing
We seek, can be secure
Unless we seek it for all men
With spirits pure

From selfishness, indifference,
Suspicion, fear, and greed.
Teach us to seek thy blessings, Lord,
For all men's need.

Give us the holy hunger,
Give us the righteous thirst
That we, in all our seeking,
May seek thee first.

Father, we seek thy blessings of health, and satisfying work, and peaceful rest. We ask thy gifts of stimulating thought, the understanding of family and friends, and the full supplying of our needs. May all these blessings which we seek for ourselves be given equally to people of all races and nations. May we never seek thy blessings at the expense of others. In Christ's name. AMEN.

V. WHATEVER IS LOVELY

Consider the lilies of the field, how they grow; they neither toil nor spin; yet I tell you, even Solomon in all his glory was not arrayed like one of these. But if God so clothes the grass of the field, which today is alive and tomorrow is thrown into the oven, will he not much more clothe you, O men of little faith?

—Matt. 6:28-30

TENACIOUS IS THE HEART

Whatever loveliness the heart has found
It will remember. Shaken with distress,
And wild with weeping, it recalls the sound
Of thrushes' song in twilight loneliness,

And is not desolate. Beset by new
Dismay, or heavy with familiar woe,
It finds relief in unforgotten dew
On little leaves, where little breezes blow.

Tenacious is the heart of every frail
Least loveliness the stricken must not miss
Lest faith should perish. Delicate its scale
Of balances whereon one instant's bliss

Of petals shaken from an April tree
Outweighs uncounted hours of agony.

O God, our heavenly Father, we thank thee that thou hast created loveliness in all things large and small. We thank thee for each remembered glimpse of beauty that has brought comfort and reassurance when we have been tempted to doubt thy care for us. Sustain our faith, O God, in the times of testing, and clothe our hearts in loveliness as thou dost clothe the lilies of the field. In Christ's name. AMEN.

GRAPE LEAVES

You haven't noticed grape leaves in the springtime?
They're heart-shaped, faintly green, with notched pink **edges**,
The whole leaf flushed with pink, and yet it's green—
You know how nature hints at several things
While saying one. The leaf is thick to touch.
It's not a glossy feel, but soft and warm;
The small, soft leaves protect the little buds,
Wee pink-tipped promises of blooms and grapes.
Grape leaves are things most folks don't seem to know
Like lilacs, and the other springtime joys,
But looking at them's reason for delight.
A grape vine in the spring's a seemly sight.

Dear Lord, whose poet-king considered thy heavens and was filled with awe, whose Son bade us consider the lilies and the ravens and have faith in thee, forgive us that we are a people who do not know and do not consider. Teach us to take time each day to stop and consider the great wonders and the small perfections of thy world, till rest and peace come to our hurried hearts. In Christ's name. AMEN.

And God said, "Let the earth put forth vegetation, plants yielding seed, and fruit trees bearing fruit in which is their seed, each according to its kind, upon the earth." And it was so. The earth brought forth vegetation, plants yielding seed according to their own kinds, and trees bearing fruit in which is their seed, each according to its kind. And God saw that it was good.

—Gen. 1:11-12

"AND GOD SAID"

It must have been
A lovelier word
Than the ears of men
Have ever heard—

The word God said
That made the tall
Strength of the trunk,
And the boughs, and all

The rich designs
Of pure delight
Of leaves, that still
On a silent night,

Reminded by
Some passing breeze
Echo the word
That made the trees.

We praise thee, Lord, for the sturdy grace of trees in silhouette against a winter sky, and for the cool blessing of their shade from summer suns. We praise thee for the beauty of their blossoms, and for the goodness of their fruit. We praise thee, Father, for all that the rich loveliness of trees has meant to us through all our days. In Christ's name. AMEN.

And God made the two great lights, the greater light to rule the day, and the lesser light to rule the night; he made the stars also. . . . And God said, "Let the waters bring forth swarms of living creatures, and let birds fly above the earth across the firmament of the heavens."   —Gen. 1:16, 20

BOUNTY

God could have left the sky
Empty of wings,
Empty of lilting
Swift motion that sings.

White stars to measure by,
Clouds, sun, and moon;
Grace need have added
No lovelier boon.

But out of his bounty
He uttered sure words,
Fulfilling the heavens
By giving the birds.

Father of bounties, we are joyously grateful to thee for the bright cheerfulness of birds that sing glad songs without anxiety, and launch themselves on long flights through unknown skies without a hint of fear. Teach us, Lord, to trust ourselves to thy limitless love with the happy freedom of a bird exploring space. In the name of our Lord. AMEN.

The Lord is good to all,
and his compassion is over all
that he has made.
—Ps. 145:9

APRIL PRAYER

Two brown-flecked eggs blown from a hidden nest;
Two mockingbirds whose songs will not attest
That it is good to live, with ardent zest.

In the bright prodigality of spring
It will not matter that some never sing,
That myriad seeds come to no flowering.

And yet with song and blossom everywhere
I breathe upon the shining April air
One wistfully believing April prayer,

That, since the Father marks the sparrow's fall,
No stillborn song, or flower, or thought at all
Be ever wholly lost, beyond recall.

God of compassion, God of all the lost and unregarded of the
earth, teach us compassionate and thoughtful ways. Grant that no
song be stilled or any good dream lost because of our unsympa-
thetic carelessness. Awaken our concern for those whose hearts
are wounded and whose faith is failing, and teach us how to help
them, in gentleness and love. In Christ's name. AMEN.

The Son of man came to seek and to save the lost.—Luke 19:10

INTERCESSION

Lord of the resurrection,
For all who doubt today
In bitterness of spirit
And loneliness, I pray.

For all who weep, like Mary,
For all who walk in fear—
Oh, with thy radiant presence
Draw near to them, draw near.

To hearts bowed down with sorrow,
To souls in desperate need,
O grant the joyous knowledge
That Christ is risen indeed.

Father of infinite caring, we pray for all who do not pray to thee, who have never known or have forgotten thee. Be with them, Lord, in mercy and in blessing, and draw them to thyself with cords of love, that they may have peace and joy and rich, abundant life. In the name of the Savior. AMEN.

The hills gird themselves with joy,
the meadows clothe themselves with flocks,
the valleys deck themselves with grain,
they shout and sing together for joy.
　　　　　　　　　　—Ps. 65:12-13

MAPLE FLAME

I think, each year, it cannot be as lovely
As I remember it, since memory
Of beauty seen is half a wistful longing
For beauty that our eyes may never see;

A loneliness for some eternal splendor,
Some ultimate delight our eyes desire
Of which the loveliest things of earth are only
Inconstant symbols, fleeting as wildfire.

But, oh, this wildfire flaming on my maple!
I gaze again at glory so supreme
It seems the hue of realized aspiration,
The color of a consummated dream,

And find this radiance, fleetingly relit,
Far lovelier than I remembered it.

We praise thee, Lord of glory, for the autumn splendor of gold and crimson leaves upon the trees, lovely beyond our power to remember or to imagine. We thank thee that autumn's vivid colors and crisp, invigorating air quicken us to work with renewed enthusiasm for the fulfillment of bright possibilities. In Christ's name. AMEN.

The heavens are the Lord's heavens,
  but the earth he has given to the sons of men.
                                    —Ps. 115:16

MUTED DAY

This is a muted day, a day for being
As quiet as the noiseless clouds that show
The earth to us, prohibiting our seeing
The sky. This is a day for us to know

Anew, the undulations of our land,
The variously corrugated bark
Of trees, and many things so near at hand
We overlook them. Now we may remark

Upon our three Nandina bushes bearing
Both red and shining silver berries, long
After the rain has ceased, and gaily sharing
Them with small feathered instruments of song.

This is a day when clouds make earth appear
Especially intimate, especially dear.

Lord, we thank thee that there is loveliness in the clouded days
as well as in the fair ones. Teach us, we pray, to seek for and
perceive the good in every situation. Keep us from assuming that
there are only a few kinds of beauty and only a few sorts of goodness, and from limiting our approval to these few. Grant us joyous
appreciation of the rich diversity of life, and make us eager to try
all things and hold fast that which is good. In Christ's name. AMEN.

O Lord, how manifold are thy works!
In wisdom hast thou made them all.
—Ps. 104:24

TRUST IN RICHES

In earliest youth I thought that I must gaze
At beauty hungrily, with greedy eyes,
Lest any fleeting loveliness escape
Of leaf or wing or opal evening skies
Before my heart could wholly memorize
A rainbow's coloring, a cloudlet's shape.

With longer living, I have grown more wise.
I look at beauty gently, without strain
Of terror lest I lose it, having learned
Beauty received with gladness will remain
And that, from earth's great undiminished store
There will be always more, and more, and more.

O God, who hast given us richly all things to enjoy, we praise
thee for the abundance and the variety of thy gifts. Help us to
remember, Lord, that thou hast given the earth to us to till and
to keep. Help us to use it wisely and conscientiously, so that there
may be always more of sustenance and beauty for those who follow
us. In Christ's name. AMEN.

The hearing ear and the seeing eye,
the Lord has made them both.
—Prov. 20:12

A PRAYER FOR SEEING EYES

Lord, I would ask, indeed, for seeing eyes
For the rich world of beauty thou hast made,
For all variety and glad surprise
Of bud and blossom, storm and sun and shade.

Lord, I would never be like those who pass
Unseeingly, the myriad tender hints
Of thee in small leaf-shadows on new grass
And in a dawn sky's pearly lustrous tints.

But grant, Lord, that I may perceive, as well,
Thy beauty in tired faces, weary hands,
The hurt and need that lips will never tell
Except to one who sees and understands.

Lord, most of all I ask for eyes to see
When anyone has any need of me.

Father in heaven, help us to be responsive to the feelings and needs
of others. Help us to sense when they are tired and depressed, and
to know the right and gentle thing to say and do. May we neither
intrude on others with unasked advice, nor unwittingly discourage
any who would confide in us. Give us, O God, the gift of healing
love for others' needs. In Christ's name. AMEN.

VI. Whatever Is Gracious

Every good endowment and every perfect gift is from above, coming down from the Father of lights with whom there is no variation or shadow due to change. —Jas. 1:17

NOT BY CHANCE

In every heart there are a hundred questions
Concerning how our living might have gone
If we had heeded all the small suggestions
That came to us, before we hurried on—

If we had taken that path, returned that call,
Answered that letter on the day it came,
Would it have made a difference, after all,
Or would our living be about the same?

This much is sure, a minor circumstance
Can alter life and make it rich or poor,
And I am certain it was not by chance
You wrote, and not by chance I answered your

Good letter on the day it came to me.
This friendship, it is clear, was meant to be.

O gracious Father, giver of every perfect gift, we thank thee for the blessing of good friends. We confess that we have often been more concerned with things than with people, and so have missed opportunities for giving and for receiving helpful friendship. Forgive us, Lord, for being too busy to receive the gifts that thou wouldst give; help us to be sensitive and obedient to thy guidance at all times. In Christ's name. AMEN.

Accept, I pray you, my gift that is brought to you, because God has dealt graciously with me, and because I have enough.

—Gen. 33:11

MEETINGS

There is a silent question
Whenever strangers meet;
All hearts, except the largest,
Persistently repeat:

Are you the good companion
I've always sought, to be
A wisely understanding
And loyal friend to me?

Our hearts are eager, seeking;
But selfless hearts transcend
The question, saying clearly:
I am your friend.

Thou knowest, Lord, how much concerned we are with our own desires and needs, and how we seek for those who may satisfy them. Thou knowest how difficult it is for us to think of others first. Transform our spirits, Lord. Help us so to live with thee and to learn of thee that we may spontaneously offer friendship to those we meet, because thou hast filled our hearts to overflowing. In Christ's name. AMEN.

CORRESPONDENT

Her letters always mention flowers blooming.
"The amaryllis looks so happy now,"
She writes on soggy winter days, assuming
We'll know it's indoor blossoms that endow

Her small neat rooms with joy. "The little pink
African violets look like baby Joan.
I'll take them to old Nancy soon, I think.
It's selfish to enjoy them all alone."

In sunny seasons, talk of daffodils,
And salvia, the hummingbirds' delight,
And roses, sunflowers, and chrysanthemums fills
The pages of each letter she must write.

She does not mention dark and lonely hours,
For she is one who reckons time by flowers.

We thank thee, heavenly Father, for all the people who are brave in small unnoticed ways, who are cheerful when they might more easily be sad, who rejoice in thy gifts instead of spending their days in regretting their losses. Help us, O God, so to appreciate the least of all thy blessings in our lives that we may ever give a good report to others. In Christ's name. AMEN.

He has caused his wonderful works to be remembered;
the Lord is gracious and merciful.

—Ps. 111:4

CAMP MEMORY

There was a shy trail
Leading us far
Up the green mountain
To camp by a star.

There was a bright fire
Leaping, proud,
And a young moon
Cocooned in cloud.

There was a pine wind
For lullaby,
And a white bird
In the dawn sky.

There was enchantment
That will be
Ours as long
As memory.

We are grateful, Lord, for memories of beautiful and gracious
hours; we are grateful for good things to think about. Help us to
use wisely the wonderful power of memory; help us to notice and
remember the lovely sights we see, the kind things people do, and
the helpful words we hear. Guard us from dwelling on and driving
deep into our minds the unkind acts and thoughtless words of
others, and keep us from acts and words which it would hurt us
and others to recall. In Christ's name. AMEN.

70

In peace I will both lie down and sleep;
for thou alone, O Lord, makest me dwell in safety.
—Ps. 4:8

THIS SILENT HOUR

What shall I choose of all this pleasant day
For dreaming on, now that the day is past?
What is most worthy to be put away
In silver-tissued sleep, that it may last

While memory remains? A single rose
Filled all the air with sweetness; one sure word
Most gently spoken, brought a new repose
To anxious faces; far away a bird

Sang through dim twilight softly; winds came blowing
To us from hills where trysting pines are tall
As newly-lighted stars. So much was glowing
With purest loveliness; but, after all,

This silent hour that blesses all the rest
With thankfulness to thee, Lord—this is best.

Dear Lord, while we remember and give thanks for the blessings of our day, we would remember also those who lack the blessings thou hast given us. Lord, be with all the ill, the lonely, the worried, and the sorrowing people, and give them healing peace, comfort, and quiet rest. And graciously bless and sustain all who work through the hours of darkness for our good. In Christ's name. AMEN.

I have a goodly heritage.—Ps. 16:6

GOLD MEMORY

That morning the leaves were purer, clearer gold
Than I have ever seen them since that day.
My sister wore a blue dress and a yellow sweater
Under the trees, with the golden light at play

Happily in her hair. The golden light
Was good to her. My blue-eyed mother stood
Beside me, where my earth-brown father came.
She smiled at him, and the golden light was good

To all of us. It is little enough to remember
Vividly, out of all of life's loss and endeavor,
But the leaves were purely, clearly, perfectly gold,
And I wanted that moment to go on forever.

We thank thee, heavenly Father, for moments of heightened
sensitivity when we become poignantly aware of the glory of thy
world and of the dearness of those whom we love. Help us in our
darkest times to remember these transcendant moments, Lord, so
that we may never lose faith in the ultimate goodness of life. In
Christ's name. AMEN.

He will surely be gracious to you at the sound of your cry; when he hears it, he will answer you. —Isa. 30:19

IN SADNESS

What shall I do, O Father, with this sadness?
Is there a use that I can put it to?
Has it a necessary work to do?

O God, the heavy weight of hopeless yearning,
The drooping heart, the spent and strengthless nerve—
Teach me, O teach me, Lord, how these can serve.

If they serve but to make my heart more tender,
More quick in sympathy with those who weep,
Or have no tears, grief being still and deep;

If they serve but to make my spirit stronger
For bearing the dark burden, as I must,
With patience and humility and trust—

Then it is well. But let this sadness not
Be wasted in self-pity. Let it be
Somehow, O Lord, of service unto thee.

O God, be with us in our sorrow, strengthen us in our weakness, help us to trust thee when we cannot understand. Grant that in our disasters we may not turn from thee in rebellious bitterness. Grant that we may not despair in the monotonous desert stretches of our lives, when there seems no purpose, no achievement, and no help, but only the thankless doing of irksome tasks. O Father, keep us faithful always unto thee. In Christ's name. AMEN.

Therefore, my beloved brethren, be steadfast, immovable, always abounding in the work of the Lord, knowing that in the Lord your labor is not in vain. —I Cor. 15:58

DISTANT STAR

I can't be sure the star I think I see
Tonight, is shining now. It well may be,

Since this calm benison of tranquil light
Has traveled myriad years to reach my sight,

The star which seems so brightly beautiful
Is now in total darkness, cold and dull—

A thought with power to illuminate
The mind, a gracious thought to contemplate.

When nothing seems to come of all the good
I try to do, I'm glad I've understood

That nights may still be lighted by the glow
Of stars that perished centuries ago.

Save us, our Father, from discouragement, the deadliest enemy of any good. Help us patiently to persevere even in hours of disillusionment and weariness. Help us to be steadfast, Father, in our conviction that all the good we try to do bears fruit somewhere, somehow, whether or not we ever see the harvest. And grant us to be content with this. Through Christ our Lord. AMEN.

And the angel said to them, "Be not afraid; for behold, I bring
you good news of a great joy which will come to all the people; for
to you is born this day in the city of David a Savior, who is Christ
the Lord."   —Luke 2:10-11

I WISH YOU CHRISTMAS

How strangely, thoughtlessly unnecessary
It often seems to me that we should say,
"I wish you merry Christmas." How can merry
Or any other adjective, convey

A wish for greater gladness for our friends
More than the one word, Christmas, all alone,
The singing, shining word that comprehends
The utmost grace and glory men have known?

I wish you more, much more, than merriment;
All faith and hope and love and holy peace,
All quietness and radiant content
With blessings that continuously increase,

And when I say the simple words and small,
"I wish you Christmas," I have wished you all.

Father in heaven, we praise thee for the holy and most gracious
gift of Christ our Savior. Let Christmas ever be to us a day of
reverent joy and worship. Fill our hearts, O Father, with the spirit
of peace and good will and brotherhood, of forgiveness and generosity and loving concern for all who are in need; and let it not
be for us a spirit of one day only but for every day of all our lives.
In his name. AMEN.

In him was life, and the life was the light of men. The light shines in the darkness, and the darkness has not overcome it.
—John 1:4-5

UNLESS IT ECHOED STILL

How should we sing, unless it echoed still
Within our hearts, the heavenly antheming
The shepherds heard on dark Judean hill—
Unless it echoed still, how should we sing?

How should we find our way, unless it burned
Within our hearts, the star with flaming ray
That led Wise Men to him for whom they yearned—
Unless it burned, how should we find our way?

How should we live, unless the Christ had birth
Within our hearts at Christmastime, to give
Singing and light and life to all on earth—
Unless the Christ had birth, how should we live?

O God, our hearts grow faint when we think of what our lives would be if Christ had not come and spoken to us the words of life and light. We thank thee that he taught us to call thee Father; we thank thee that he gives song instead of discord, and light instead of darkness, and life instead of death. We thank thee, heavenly Father, in his name. AMEN.

VII. If There Is Any Excellence

When Jesus heard this he marveled at him.—Luke 7:9

GOD'S MARVELOUS PEOPLE

How often have I marveled at the deep
Humility and faith of one I know
Who, having cause, in all her days, to weep,
Has never let her laughter rust, and so

Continuously conquers, and I look
With marveling and loving eyes at one
Who, in her darkest season, undertook
To do not only what had to be done,

But countless generous, thoughtful acts as well.
I marvel at the beauty God has made
In all this gracious earth on which we dwell,
Vast hills, and joyous light, and gentle shade;

But the richest cause for praise I always find
In lives of people who are brave and kind.

Father in heaven, we thank thee for all the faith and fortitude, for all the generosity and kindness, in the lives of the people we know. We thank thee for the daily goodness in the lives of unknown and unregarded people. Grant that we may never judge any person as having little good in him; help us to remember that Christ marveled at the faith, and the generous concern for others, which he found in unexpected places. In his name. AMEN.

Abound more and more, with knowledge and all discernment, so that you may approve what is excellent. —Phil. 1:9-10

VISITOR TO THE MOUNTAINS

"How can these mountain people live," she asks,
"Amid this mountain grandeur, never showing
The least appreciation, at their tasks,
Of the sight of a million dogwood blossoms blowing

In spring? They seem too stolid to perceive
How mountain sunsets make one's spirit tall.
These people have, I really do believe,
No finer sensibilities at all."

I looked at tired, work-silent folk with thin
Enduring faces, whose incessant toil
In storm and heat and drought, can barely win
A scant subsistence from this mountain soil,

And thought, *What sensibility denies
A grandeur more than mountains' in their eyes?*

O Thou who hast compassion on all who labor and are heavy laden, help us to value well the uncomplaining patience of their lives. Give us discernment to see beyond appearances to the beauty that lies in the silent endurance of hardship, and in the flowering of gentleness and love among the frosts of poverty and disappointment. In the name of Christ. AMEN.

I was a son with my father,
tender, the only one in the sight of my mother.
—Prov. 4:3

FUNERAL FOR A SON

They rose before dawn stumbled up the sky
Just as they always had. He milked, and fed
The stock while she got breakfast just for two.
"I never will get used to it," she said.
Then neither spoke. She washed up the few dishes,
And then, like prisoners hopeless of release,
They sat there slowly waiting while the sun
Crawled up the brazen sky on hands and knees.
So short a time, she thought, we had a son.
We have a wire of war's polite regrets.
I wonder how it is we keep on dying.
It hurts as much each time the heart forgets
A moment, and remembers—"Time to go."
"The sun's so bright. It should be dark and gray,"
She answered dully. Kindly folk at church
Said all they could. There wasn't much to say.
"I am the resurrection and the life."
It's long to wait, she thought. It's long to wait.
Then they were home. They couldn't seem to stir.
"I might as well go milk. It's getting late,"
He said at last. She said, "I'll fix some supper,"
For two, she thought; but found a smile to give.
You go on dying while you wait to die,
You go on living while you wait to live.

'trengthen, O God, all hearts that are maimed by war, and hasten
he day when wars forever cease. In Christ's name. AMEN.

79

Be of good courage, and he shall strengthen thine heart.
—Ps. 27:14, K.J.V.

OF COURAGE

I have loved courage; I have loved the word,
Its look on any printed page, its shape
On any lips, its meaning, clear, unblurred,
In weathered faces, seeking no escape

In bitterness from bitter circumstances,
And I have loved it in the candid mind
That, scorning easy falsities, advances
Toward truth, however seemingly unkind.

I have loved well each winter-blooming flower
And each gaunt, stubborn, twisted tree, that brought
New courage to me in a desperate hour;
For, loving courage, I have always sought

For it in everything that I have known,
Because I have scant courage of my own.

O thou who knowest all our inmost fears and weaknesses, we
thank thee that as we seek for the courage we need, thou dost ever
strengthen our hearts. Help us, our Father, to know that we may
always measure up to our highest ideals of truth and honesty, even
when this requires more courage than we possess. For thou, Lord,
wilt supply us with courage according to our willingness to use it.
Through Christ our Lord. AMEN.

With thee is the fountain of life;
in thy light do we see light.
—Ps. 36:9

THE SOURCE

"Some day," she said, "when I have less to do,
I'm going to follow yonder chuckling stream
Clear back into the hills, and learn the source
Of music that has laughter for its theme.

"And then," she said, "when I am not so tired,
I'm going to climb up to the tallest peak
Of the very highest hill, and learn the source
Of beauty never daunted, never weak."

But she was always busy, often tired,
And since she never traveled any length
From home, we wondered how she found the source
Of laughing music and undaunted strength.

Our Father, preserve us, we pray, from the futility of seeking the source of life and joy in distant places or in outward things. Give us sure faith that we have within ourselves, if our lives are joined to thee through obedient prayer, the strength for overcoming difficulty and for releasing harmony and beauty where we are. In Christ's name. AMEN.

The wisdom from above is first pure, then peaceable, gentle, open to reason, full of mercy and good fruits, without uncertainty or insincerity.
—Jas. 3:17

HERMANN OF REICHENAU
(1013–54)

Within the convent walls his spirit shone
One of the darkened ages' purest lights.
He who could neither walk nor stand alone
Wrote treatises on measuring the heights

Of stars; translated Aristotle; penned
The world's known history in scrupulous pages;
And he, whose maimed speech none could comprehend,
Composed *Come, Holy Spirit,* for the ages.

In constant suffering gentle, brave, and kind,
In reverent eagerness for truth and learning,
He kept the records of the questing mind,
And voiced the heart's deep love and holy yearning,

And all the clouded centuries have not dimmed
His luminous spirit or the faith he hymned.

We thank thee, heavenly Father, for those through all the ages who by their devotion to good preserved for us the heritage of faith, truth, and knowledge, and who added to it their own lives' shining examples of virtue and excellence. May we, who inherit the treasures they preserved, possess their fidelity, their radiance, and their holy curiosity. In Christ's name. AMEN.

Recall the former days.—Heb. 10:32

REMEMBERING ONES

Those who have not forgotten the sick pain
They felt, as children, at strange grown-up laughter
At serious matters, are the ones who gain
Children's respect, and keep it ever after.

Those who remember vividly their numb
Defenseless misery at a smile, a word,
And the frantic depths the untried heart can plumb,
Do not treat youthful ardor as absurd.

And it is they, the rare, remembering ones,
Whose gentle sympathy sustains the tall,
Uncertain youngsters, when derision stuns
Their eager zest. It would be well if all

Those who were young, not very long ago,
Could be reminded of the things they know.

Help us, heavenly Father, to remember the idealism of youthful
hearts and their vulnerability to indulgent scorn. Help us to
cherish young people's enthusiasm for high causes and great
enterprises. Help us to remember that the hope of the future rests
on their capacity for complete dedication to thy work, and their
ability to feel selfless anger at injustice and wrong. In Christ's
name. AMEN.

. . . well attested for her good deeds, as one who has brought up children, shown hospitality, washed the feet of the saints, relieved the afflicted, and devoted herself to doing good in every way.

—I Tim. 5:10

AFTERTHOUGHT

"We should have planted shrubs," she said.
"That wouldn't need a lot of care.
Crepe myrtle, lilac, flowering quince—
I know the place looks awfully bare.

"But we were busy all the years
With raising children—ours, and then
Manette's four boys. All grown and gone.
All grown, we think, into fine men.

"And we are hardly able now
To care for flowers. We're getting on.
But we never thought the place looked bare
Until the boys were grown and gone."

Dear Lord, we thank thee for all the people who do thy work, in self-forgetful love, through crowded years. We pray that thy richest blessings may abound to those who give a mother's tenderness and a father's care to children who are homeless and bereft. May their sacrifices bear a deeply satisfying harvest in the upright, useful lives of devoted sons and daughters. In Christ's name. AMEN.

And they came, bringing to him a paralytic carried by four men. And when they could not get near him because of the crowd, they removed the roof above him; and when they had made an opening, they let down the pallet on which the paralytic lay. And when Jesus saw their faith, he said to the paralytic, "My son, your sins are forgiven. . . . Rise, take up your pallet and go home." And he rose, and immediately took up the pallet and went out before them all.
—Mark 2:3-5, 11-12

THE UNNAMED FOUR

I like to think of them, the unnamed four,
Who, finding crowds too dense about the door
For easy entrance, did not turn away
Murmuring, "We tried, at least—another day,
Perhaps—" who did not rudely push and shove
A path through thronging people, but with love
For their good friend determining them that he
Must meet the One who, certainly, could be
Of help to him, sought stubbornly till one
Of them discovered how it could be done—
"We'll let his bed down through the roof!" And so
It was accomplished. That is all we know
About the unnamed four. Did Jesus speak
To them, or only smile? They did not seek
Help for themselves from him, or any praise,
But they must have remembered his clear gaze,
And, seeing their good friend walking tall and strong,
Walked taller than before, their whole lives long.

Father, we thank thee for the people who seek nothing for themselves, and who diligently persevere in their efforts to make thy help available to others. In Christ's name. AMEN.

85

He has put down the mighty from their thrones,
and exalted those of low degree;
he has filled the hungry with good things,
and the rich he has sent empty away.

—Luke 1:52-53

A SONG FOR LONELY PEOPLE

It was a lonely journey
For those who traveled far
Beyond their known horizons;
For them there shone a star.

It was a lonely vigil
For those who watched among
Their charges in the darkness;
For them a song was sung.

It was a lonely resting
For those who met with scorn
To find reluctant shelter;
To them a child was born.

Love to all lonely people
To whom, amid the throng
Of rushing folk, are given
The starlight and the song.

Lord of the lowly and the lonely, who dost resist the proud and give grace to the humble, help us to cleanse our hearts of pride and vanity. Teach us how empty we are if we seek treasure for ourselves and are not rich toward thee. Teach us to dread no loneliness save the loneliness for thee that comes of following the crowd and not thy will. In Christ's name. AMEN.

VIII. If There Is Anything Worthy of Praise

In the days of David and Asaph of old there was a chief of the singers, and there were songs of praise and thanksgiving to God.
—Neh. 12:46

HERITAGE OF GRATITUDE

We thank thee, Lord, that men through all the ages
Have offered hearts and hymns of praise to thee.
We thank thee for the wisdom of the sages
Establishing an annual jubilee

Of gratitude for harvests, and for all
Thy changeless mercies through the changing years,
A season when we fervently recall
That thou hast helped, alike in joy and fears.

We thank thee for all who, in times of stress
And desolation and dismay, renewed
Their praise, remembering thou dost ever bless.
Ours is a heritage of gratitude,

The finest gift our fathers could impart
The lesson of the lifted, thankful heart.

Father in heaven, may we never forget thy benefits or fail to bless thy holy name. May we never presumptuously take for granted all the blessings thou hast given us, grumbling at lack of some particular blessing we desire. Keep us true to the knowledge of our fathers that worship and praise of thee is our best privilege and highest joy. In the name of Christ. Amen.

The Lord is my shepherd, I shall not want;
  he makes me lie down in green pastures.
He leads me beside still waters;
  he restores my soul.

. . . .

Surely goodness and mercy shall follow me
  all the days of my life;
and I shall dwell in the house of the Lord
  for ever.

—Ps. 23:1-3, 6

SONG

This year there will be songs to sing,
And books to read, and stars to see.
There will be April blossoming
And autumn in a maple tree.

This year there will be smoky mist
On distant hills, clouds surging by,
Sunrises, pearl and amethyst,
And wings across a sunset sky.

This year there will be work to do,
And fellowship and mirth to share,
And challenges to meet, and new
Adventures of the heart to dare.

This year, this year my heart shall lift
On wings of joy, on wings of praise,
In gratitude for God's great gift,
The boundless miracle of days.

We thank thee, Lord, for the gift of life, for the opportunity to love, to learn, to grow, and to become what thou wouldst have us be. Help us ever to use the time thou givest us to good account. Through Christ our Lord. AMEN.

THE SACRIFICE OF PRAISE

If we would offer praise
To God continually
Our hearts must sacrifice
Some things that seem to be
Peculiarly dear;
The pleasure of complaining
When little things go wrong
And little hurts are paining;
The joy of feeling abused
And envious of our neighbors,
And sorry for ourselves
And our unrequited labors;
The pride of pointing out
The small defects that mar
Our satisfactions, to prove
How skilled in taste we are—
All this the heart intent
On offering praise, foregoes,
And, sacrificing, finds
All freedom and repose.
And yet by some perverse
And curious mistake
It seems a sacrifice
Our hearts are loath to make.

Lord, we would be patient in our trials and tribulations. But keep us from priding ourselves on our patience in nonexistent trials and imaginary tribulations. Give us always a sense of proportion and a spirit of praise. In Christ's name. AMEN.

Rejoice always, pray constantly, give thanks in all circumstances; for this is the will of God in Christ Jesus for you.

—I Thess. 5:16-18

THE ONE THING

Sometimes, perplexed and shaken,
Uncertain of His will,
In dread lest my mistaken
Unguided act bring ill,

I find I've been remiss
In the one thing I must do:
"Rejoice, give thanks, for this
Is the will of God for you."

So, letting go the worry
That made my spirit dim,
The pressure and the hurry,
I offer praise to him

In fullness of thanksgiving
That he who keeps our days
Wills that each hour of living
Be full of joy and praise.

And while my heart rejoices
In his great love, I find
The hard, perplexing choices
Grow clear within my mind.

Father, we thank thee that thou hast given us one certain guide to what thou wouldst have us do in every time and place. Forgive us that in eagerness to do what seems to us some greater thing, we forget the one thing needful and become confused and tense. Teach us, in all perplexities, to turn to thee in praise. In Christ's name. AMEN.

90

Though the fig tree do not blossom, . . .
and the fields yield no food, . . .
yet I will rejoice in the Lord.
                                    —Hab. 3:17-18

MISSED

"It's raining at Jackson's!
It's raining, my dear!"
Mom looked at Dad dully.
"It hasn't rained here."

Jim came in. "It's pouring
At Smith's—and that's near.
But I see"—his face twisted—
"It hasn't rained here."

"Without rain, we'll have nothing—
Just nothing—next year."
"I know it." "Seems curious
It hasn't rained here."

"Look off over yonder
How fresh things appear.
It's rained all around,
But it hasn't rained here."

"We ought to be thankful"—
Mom's voice wasn't clear—
"Our neighbors got rain,
Though it hasn't rained here."

Create in us, O God, hearts that sincerely rejoice in the good that comes to others, even though it be withheld from us. In Christ's name. AMEN.

The Lord your God is bringing you into a good land, a land of brooks of water, of fountains and springs, flowing forth in valleys and hills, a land of wheat and barley, of vines and fig trees and pomegranates, a land of olive trees and honey, a land in which you will eat bread without scarcity, in which you will lack nothing, a land whose stones are iron, and out of whose hills you can dig copper. And you shall eat and be full, and you shall bless the Lord your God for the good land he has given you. —Deut. 8:7-10

IN THIS OUR LAND

Always something escapes the frost,
Always something escapes the heat.
In spite of reports that the crops are lost
There is always sufficient for us to eat.

Always something escapes the flood,
Always something escapes the drought.
Never the lifeless seed and bud,
The shriveled body, the empty mouth.

Out of our varied, ample lands
Always enough, for us, and to spare.
Lord of our overflowing hands,
May we be always eager to share.

O God, we praise thee for the vast fertility of the land thou hast given us. We thank thee that, though we have used it with wasteful greed, its rich resources still supply our needs abundantly. Forgive us, Lord, for the arrogance we often show, as if our special righteousness or the might of our hands alone had gotten us this wealth. May we offer thanks by freely sharing all thou givest us. In Christ's name. AMEN.

92

One man gives freely, yet grows all the richer;
  another withholds what he should give, and only suffers want.
                                                    —Prov. 11:24

THANKSGIVING PRAYER

Let us be always good receivers, Lord,
Accepting with abundant gratitude
All the abundant wealth of goodness stored
In daily life, as constantly renewed

As sunlight and the fresh replenishing
Of rain; teach us to use thy gifts with free
Delight, as earth does sun and rain, to bring
Beauty to all, and joy, and harmony.

Let us be good receivers, knowing well
That those who hoard the blessings of the days
In anxious fear of need, and do not dwell
In the glad atmosphere of fervent praise

For the rich gifts of living, large and small,
Have never truly owned those gifts at all.

Father in heaven, forgive us for storing the surplus bounties of our
fields in warehouses instead of sending them to the hungry people
of other lands. Forgive us for spending extravagant amounts on
flashy luxuries and harmful amusements, and little on finding ways
to eliminate the shadow of starvation from the peoples of the
earth. Help us, in the spirit of Christ our Lord, to give freely as
we have received. AMEN.

He did not leave himself without witness, for he did good and gave you from heaven rains and fruitful seasons, satisfying your hearts with food and gladness. —Acts 14:17

IN TIME OF HARVEST

Lord of all rain and sunlight,
Lord of all grain and grass,
Lord of all constant mercies
As seasons come and pass,

Our praise for rain and sunlight,
Our praise for grass and grain,
And for thy constant mercies
That tirelessly sustain

Us through the passing seasons
And keep us strong and whole,
Supplying all our hungers
Of body and of soul.

May the deep strength of our spirits
And of our bodies be
Completely dedicated,
Our God, to serving thee.

Help us, O God, to reverence thy gifts to us of time, health, and intelligence too much to squander them on vain pursuits. Keep us alike from aimless idleness, and from undertaking more in work or play than we can healthfully and competently perform. Help us to discipline our minds to think clearly and constructively, that we may not only choose wisely between evil and good, but may choose the difficult and lonely best instead of either. AMEN.

Be still, and know that I am God.—Ps. 46:10

STILL KNOWING

I never formulated any phrase
Of gratitude for rainbows arching over
An April land of apple bloom and clover.

Glad wonder held me still, on July days,
When air grown languorous and overwarm
Received tumultuous freshenings of storm.

When all the gold and scarlet leaves were praise
Made visible on an October hill,
In ardent exultation I was still.

And when in calm December skies my gaze
Perceived the one most brightly shining star,
There was a glory words could only mar.

But thou, O Father of the silent ways,
Received my deepest thanks for moments glowing
With deep, revealing silences of knowing.

We thank thee, heavenly Father, for moments when we are most
feelingly aware of thee. Teach us to wait upon thee in stillness and
tranquility of spirit, in trustful gratitude, so that even amid outward
turmoil we remain at rest with thee. Teach us to stay our minds
on thee, that we may know thy perfect peace and share with hurt
and worried hearts thy healing calm. In Christ's name. AMEN.

95

What shall I render to the Lord
*   for all his bounty to me?*
I will lift up the cup of salvation
*   and call on the name of the Lord,*
I will pay my vows to the Lord
*   in the presence of all his people.*
—Ps. 116:12-14

BENEFICENCE

Lord, how shall any soul live tall
Enough to recompense
For all the gracious gifts that flow
From thy beneficence?

Whose worth has earned one autumn tree,
Or white bird winging high,
And who has merited the sun,
Who has deserved the sky?

And to what soul of all the world,
O Father, dost thou owe
The merciful forgiving grace,
The healing love we know?

Our Father, thou hast given us all, and we can give thee only
ourselves, the love and praise of our hearts and the service of our
lives. Forgive us for our half-hearted acceptance of thy gifts, and
for our half-hearted giving of ourselves. O thou who givest all, give
us the grace to live for thee and serve thee. Through Christ our
Lord. AMEN.